Endorsements for *Overcoming GIANTS in Your Life*

OVERCOMING GIANTS IN YOUR LIFE by Brian Jennings is a must-read! Drawing inspiration from the story of David and Goliath, Jennings provides a fresh perspective on the familiar tale. He is an excellent storyteller, and his writing style is engaging and accessible. He has a talent for taking complex concepts and distilling them into simple, actionable steps that readers can follow. He is a gifted and wise pastor, and his insights are both inspiring and practical. If you are struggling with fear, doubt, or uncertainty, this book will help you to find the strength and courage to face your giants and overcome them.

Overall, I highly recommend this book for anyone who is looking to overcome obstacles and limitations in their life. Jennings reminds us that even the greatest heroes of the Bible had to overcome challenges and limitations, and that we too can achieve great things if we have faith and trust in God.

— **Vladimir Savchuk**
Pastor of Hungry Generation Church, Author of *Break Free*

If you are wondering how to defeat obstacles in your life, this is the book for you. Pastor Brian Jennings teaches you how to use the Word of God as a sword to overcome any giant that comes at you. This book embodies the scripture Rev. 12:11, "They triumphed over him by the blood of the Lamb and by the word of their testimony." His experiences make this book relatable, so that anyone is empowered to go from glory to glory.

Daniel Adams
Founder of The Supernatural Life, Author of *Supernatural Living*

An exceptional book including biblical guidelines to overcome the giants in our lives when the odds are against us. This stirred my soul, sharpened my focus, and was hard to put down. Pastor Brian experienced more trauma in his first nineteen years than most experience in a lifetime. Pastor Brian shares the biblical principles that have sustained him to maintain the level as a man of God that he continually exhibits daily. These principles that he shares kept me grounded and centered during an eighteen-year career as a law enforcement officer. For that I am eternally grateful!

Jack Curtsinger

OVERCOMING GIANTS IN YOUR LIFE will give you courage to overcome the trials and fires that you'll face in life. Listening to Brian's testimonies and seeing the faithfulness of God to deliver, time and time again, as well as the wisdom that you'll gain through each page, will make this book one that you'll not want to put down.

Shane Winnings
Author of *I Will Always Overcome*

OVERCOMING GIANTS IN YOUR LIFE is an insightful manual full of biblical wisdom for overcoming the obstacles and challenges we face in life. Through the story of David and Goliath, Brian Jennings offers inspiring insights and practical tools for confronting our own giants and finding victory through faith in God. This book is a must-read for anyone seeking to overcome the obstacles that stand in the way of their God-given destiny.

Pastor Mike Signorelli
Lead Pastor V1 Church

OVERCOMING GIANTS IN YOUR LIFE by Brian Jennings is a book that will bless your life! As you read these chapters, your heart will overflow with Courage and Hope. A must-read for everyone feeling hopeless and powerless while facing giants in their life. As you read this awesome book, allow the power of the Holy Spirit to pour the oil and the wine into your fragmented soul to cleanse you, heal you, and restore you back to health.

Joey Zamora
Lead Pastor at Cornerstone Church and Founder of Better Together Ministries

OVERCOMING IN YOUR LIFE

**HOW TO STAND STRONG
WHEN THE ODDS
ARE AGAINST YOU**

GIANTS

BRIAN JENNINGS

OVERCOMING giants IN YOUR LIFE
Copyright © 2023 by Brian Jennings
Published by Brian Jennings

Brian Jennings
P.O. Box 10966
Yakima, WA 98909

Unless otherwise indicated, all Scriptures are from the NEW KING JAMES VERSION®. Copyright © 1982 by Thomas Nelson, Inc. Used by permission. All rights reserved.

Scriptures marked NAS are taken from the NEW AMERICAN STANDARD (NAS): Scripture taken from the NEW AMERICAN STANDARD BIBLE®, copyright© 1960, 1962, 1963, 1968, 1971, 1972, 1973, 1975, 1977, 1995 by The Lockman Foundation. Used by permission.

All emphases within scriptural quotations are the author's own.

All rights reserved. No part of this book may be reproduced or transmitted in any form or by any means, electronic or mechanical, including photocopying, recording, or by any information storage and retrieval system, without permission in writing from the author. Please direct your inquiries to brian@breakthroughchristian.com.

ISBNs: 979-8-9883349-0-3 (Paperback)

        979-8-9883349-1-0 (E-book)

Printed in the United States of America.

DEDICATION AND ACKNOWLEDGEMENTS

I want to dedicate this book to my family.

My wife, Kari, for your love, care, consistency, and encouragement! You have been my rock along with the Lord! I absolutely adore you! I truly would not be able to do what I do without you! Thank you for being faithful to God and me!

My three daughters: Mariah, Alexis, and Seri, for loving me and believing in me! Thank you all for helping me enjoy life more! I'm so proud of you girls!

My son-in-law, Jordan, for your encouragement! You're a miracle! I can't wait to read your book! Thank you for taking care of Mariah!

I want to acknowledge a few people that have helped change my life for the better.

These folks are Dan & Judy, who are my in-laws! They're my spiritual parents also! They have helped me more than anyone in my life! I love you both immensely!

I also want to mention my aunt Patsy and my late Uncle Sam, who raised me from the 5th through the 12th grade! You helped change my story! I love you very much, and I'll never forget what you did for me! Thank you!

Lastly, I want to thank my church family—Breakthrough Church! You have loved me and believed in me, even when I didn't believe in myself! Thank you for being real, authentic, and the God-lovers that you are! I'm a proud pastor!

CONTENTS

Foreword 11

Introduction 15

Chapter 1   Beyond Limitations 19

Chapter 2   When the Odds are Against You 27

Chapter 3   Rock Bottom 35

Chapter 4   God Encounters 43

Chapter 5   Stones and Steps 51

FOREWORD

Since Brian Jennings first mentioned this book to me, I have excitedly anticipated reading it. The challenge to *overcome limitations* is something a lot of people talk about. Voices from TED Talks and school assemblies—motivational speakers and head coaches—challenge audiences, clients, and athletes to break through barriers and move forward. And, with those influences, we all hope to overcome our own limitations; however, Brian's story is distinctive. Brian was picked by God.

I hold this opinion because I've known Brian. His story is not only jaw-dropping and perilous, but also threaded with the tapestry of a heroic rescue story. Brian's rescue, initiated by God, is something captivating that I have watched him live out. He's not only a great pastor, theologian, man of prayer, husband, father and friend; Brian is God's saved man, empowered.

I have watched him methodically take strategic steps because of Holy Spirit, process them through prayer and the Scriptures, and then bring them to a full-send through wisdom. He's done this because he's been in the dark.

OVERCOMING GIANTS IN YOUR LIFE

> For we do not wrestle against flesh and blood, but against principalities, against powers, against the rulers of t*he darkness* of this age, against spiritual hosts of wickedness in the heavenly places. (Ephesians 6:12)

When you find yourself on the brightest side of God's rescue story, you'll have looked back upon the landscape of your life and seen the darkness for what it is. Satan seeks to destroy what is and what will be. In Brian's case, he was miraculously snatched from the deception. The serpent is far more deceptive than he is capable, far more crafty than strong. And men like Brian, who know this, know our enemies who defy the living God will soon be overcome, and overrun.

> Having disarmed principalities and powers, He made a public spectacle of them, triumphing over them in it. (Colossians 2:15)

Brian knows that Jesus is King, Satan is a defeated foe, and God has unique strategies and unique weapons of our warfare. He knows there is nothing that cannot be overcome. I know it too. And I am confident, after you enjoy reading this book, you will stand taller, speak bolder, and go harder to overcome your every limitation.

FOREWORD

Brian did.

I have.

You will too.

— **Jeff Knight**
 Pastor of The Rock Church, NASCAR Driver, and Author of *The Revved Life*

INTRODUCTION

This devotional story is designed with a purpose: to equip you to overcome the giants you are facing in your life now, and those you will face in the future. In this book, my hope is that you will see things that you have never before seen in the Word of God from the story of David and Goliath—and all that David was up against (1 Samuel 17). My desire is for you to read this with an open heart, and for the Holy Spirit to clearly speak to you about your own life. I pray that you will see healing manifest in your life as you read these words of my heart, now on paper.

I would say that most of the people that God uses greatly have had to overcome some major battles in life and allow God to heal them from their past! My friend Pastor Vlad says that whatever is not transformed, or healed in our lives, will get transferred down to the next generation: our children. I have seen this in my own life and in the lives of others. Many times, the Enemy comes into our lives and whispers things like: *You haven't changed. You're not really healed. You didn't really forgive that person. You don't have victory anymore after what you have done.* I've experienced this, and chances are, so have you.

God has done a deep work in my heart and in my life, and it has brought about some incredible healing. I have been through a lot of intense stuff in my life. Three years ago, I found myself in a very dark place because I never truly healed from all of the trauma I endured in my youth. Over the last three years, the Holy Spirit has really done some heart surgery on me. I had to be willing to walk with the Lord, hand in hand, through the hard things of my past. I had to be willing to deal with my own struggles so they would not be transferred down to my kids. Three years ago, I could not even think about writing this book because I wasn't able to do it. My heart wasn't prepared to write it. I wouldn't have even known where to begin. The Holy Spirit has healed my life in a powerful way. God's timing is perfect, even when we think we know better.

In chapter five, I talk about the **five smooth stones** in my life that I used—and continue to use—as a weapon against the Enemy, and the steps that David took to overcome the giant in his life. **These fourteen steps serve as reminders to me of how I was fourteen feet away from facing my own personal Goliath—my mother's murderer—and overcame him with FORGIVENESS!**

My prayer for you is that you would see your challenges and enemies in a new light; that you will allow the Holy Spirit to walk into your past and bring clarity and

INTRODUCTION

healing; and that my story will bring you hope and the courage to fight! After all, who doesn't need hope and courage these days?

Are you ready? Let's dive in!

Chapter 1

BEYOND LIMITATIONS

In Running With The Giants by John Maxwell, I read the following: "David was limited by his earthly father, but not by his heavenly Father. When we think of David, we don't generally think of limitations. David is a man who achieved great success and made it to the top. He was a great warrior and the greatest of kings, yet there were many who never saw his potential. As a young man, he didn't look like a warrior or a king. He was the youngest in his family, and as a boy, he did not receive affirmation from those around him. David's greatest battles in his early years were not against the bear or lion he slew while protecting his father's sheep. His greatest obstacles were created by the people who tried to put limitations on him."[1]

I'm going to talk about a teenager named David because I can relate to him in many ways. He faced one-on-one the giant known as Goliath. Immediately, all of us are saying, "I know a little bit about that story."

---

1. Maxwell, John. *Running With The Giants*. New York, NY: Faith Words, 2002, 40.

OVERCOMING GIANTS IN YOUR LIFE

As well as we know this story, I'm not as interested in how the story goes as I am in learning how I can defeat giants in my own life. That's what we're going to talk about.

King Saul and the Israelites drew up to the battle lines to meet the Philistines. A champion named Goliath came out of the Philistine camp. He was over nine feet tall. Goliath said, "I defy the armies of Israel this day. Give me a man that we may fight together" (1 Samuel 17:10). When the Israelites saw Goliath, they ran from him in great fear.

> "Let me give you some historical background to help you understand why the Israeli soldiers were so afraid. The Philistines had been seafaring people who came from an island in the Middle East. Once they were settled, they established five cities that became very strong and were each led by a vicious king.
>
> "The Philistines entered the Iron Age before the Israelites did. Their weapons of war were far superior. Very notorious. The Philistines would put swords on their chariot wheels so their chariot riders could go through an infantry and mow down soldiers like you and I could cut through grass. Recently, just before

CHAPTER 1: BEYOND LIMITATIONS

this event, the Philistine army had slaughtered 30,000 Israelite soldiers in a battle. This is still fresh in the minds of these other soldiers. They were greatly afraid of the Philistines. And what the Philistines were doing on this day was not uncommon. Rather than putting their whole army into battle, the Philistines would choose one champion to go out and taunt and challenge the other army to see if they would send out one champion and these guys would go at it one on one. They would each represent their army. Whichever side won, the losing side would either retreat or surrender.

"And so the Philistines had chosen this champion well. Here is this nine-foot guy, a very skilled warrior. He had his PhD in assault and battery. Goliath was bad to the bone. He was no joke. Legit. And he's taunting and challenging the Israelite army, 'Send somebody out to fight me.' But nobody would."[2]

At this point in the story, David's not even in the picture yet. I don't know if it was because he was small or the youngest in his family, but his father had not

---
2. Hearn Travis. *Shaq Sized Problems Require God Sized Miracles*, n.d. Nov 27, 2013, Sermon Central Article

OVERCOMING GIANTS IN YOUR LIFE

allowed David to go to the front lines of battle. Only David's brothers were there. But after about thirty days, David's dad said: *We probably ought to check on the boys. Why don't you go to the front lines, carry some lunch to them, and then bring me back a report?* So, here's the teenager, lunch bucket in hand, moving toward the front lines. He hears Goliath taunting and cursing the God of Israel. David couldn't believe his ears. Why wasn't somebody doing something about this?

Our story picks up. David says to King Saul, "Let no man's heart fail because of him. Your servant will go and fight this Philistine." Saul said, "You are a youth." David said, "The LORD will deliver me from the hand of this Philistine." Walking down toward the battlefield, David pulls out a slingshot from one pocket and picks up five rocks. He puts them in the other pocket as he approaches Goliath. And Goliath said, "Am I a dog that you come to me with sticks?" He cursed David by his pagan gods. "Come here and I'll give your flesh to the birds of the air and the beasts of the field." David said, "You come against me with sword and spear and javelin." Remember the Philistines are in the Iron Age. It's estimated that the head of Goliath's spear weighed as much as a bowling ball. Goliath likely stood between nine and eleven feet tall, weighed between 500 and 600 pounds, and wore armor totaling around 230 pounds. This guy was well equipped. And David said, "That's what you come at me with, but I come against you in the name of the LORD Almighty."

CHAPTER 1: BEYOND LIMITATIONS

"This day, the LORD will hand you over to me, and the whole world will know there is a God in Israel." As Goliath moved closer to attack him, David ran quickly toward the battle line to meet him. I would have been running too, but not toward the battle line! David slung a stone and struck the Philistine. It sank into his forehead, and he fell face down on the ground. So David triumphed over Goliath with a sling and a stone. What happened next, according to the Bible, is that David walked over to the fallen corpse of the giant, removed Goliath's sword, and decapitated the giant; thus, proving that David was a man who knew how to—get ahead!

> The moments when we face our giants are the defining moments of our lives.

How can you become that courageous? How could a lion's heart of valor swell within you? All of us are going to have our giants—big things, dark things, shadows that blacken and blot out the sun. Who have your giants been? An unfaithful spouse? An abusive parent? A tyrannical boss? What have your giants been? Financial giants? Career giants? Health giants? Addiction giants? You know that the moments when we face our giants are the defining moments of our lives. In the crucible of decision, will I stand? Will I fall? Will I advance? Will I retreat? In these moments of decision, we see who we really are, and who we are becoming.

Perhaps many of you have been battling giants for a long time now. The Bible says that every day for forty days. Goliath was challenging them, taunting, and haunting them. I'm sure he was wearing them down and out. And they all just stayed back and hid, not doing a thing out of fear. They were paralyzed.

Once David showed up on the scene, it was finally time for somebody to not only say something but do something. Friend, maybe it's that time for you. Your giants have been screaming at you for too long. You see, you must deal with the giants. They must be confronted, to be defeated. Go ahead, you got this!

Personal Observation

What giant are you currently facing? It's important to name it!

_____

_____

_____

_____

CHAPTER 1: BEYOND LIMITATIONS

Personal Prayer:

Father, in the name of Jesus, I thank You that You are for me. I'm complete and accepted by You. Thank You for healing me. Thank You for always being there for me. When I feel alone, I know that You will never leave me nor forsake me. Help me to fully trust in Your goodness! Amen.

Chapter 2

WHEN THE ODDS ARE AGAINST YOU

I spent most of my childhood on the east side of Yakima, Washington, which was the ghetto of our area. I was raised between my mom and my grandparents, and several other family members who had room for me to stay with them. The reason I was in between homes so much was my mom's drug and alcohol addiction. Growing up in an environment where this was normal, led me down the wrong road very quickly. Much of what I saw growing up was people being ripped off, cheating to get ahead, and abusing drugs and everything else. Because this was all I knew, I began doing what I saw at a young age. It wasn't long before I was stealing, breaking into places, and dabbling with alcohol. By the age of ten, my life was on a downward spiral; I had spent ten days in the Juvenile Justice Center. I had a record piling up against me, and I was on a path that could have led to my life being a negative statistic.

I was not raised in church, but I remember that when I was about four years old, my grandpa would put me on the yellow Sunday school bus that would come to the east side of Yakima. I appreciate that they would pick up the kids from the hood and transport us to Sunday school to learn about God. My grandpa would give me a dollar for the offering and send me away to get rid of me for a few hours. I think it made him feel better knowing that if he wasn't going to church, at least I was. So the only relationship with God or church that I had was when I was about four years old. I went to a Seventh Day Adventist youth group a handful of times with a lady that would pick us up for church on Wednesday nights. The only reason I would go was because she promised to buy us ice cream on the way home from church. Other than that, I had no experience with church, God, or Jesus until the age of eighteen.

When I was eleven years old, I had an aunt and uncle who brought me into their family and loved me like they loved their own sons. They agreed to let me live with them because, if something didn't happen in my life, they knew I was just going to be another statistic in the city of Yakima. That's when I felt like I got to hit the reset button in my life. I remember the first couple of nights I was able to sleep in my own bed; it felt incredibly awkward because I'd never had a bed that I could call my own. For me, it was always a couch or the floor. They were good people who showed me a better way of life and taught me that I didn't have to ruin my life like so many of my family had. I thank God for them taking me in and raising me through those formative years.

CHAPTER 2: WHEN THE ODDS ARE AGAINST YOU

They raised me from the time I was in the 5th through the 12th grade and saw me graduate from Davis High School. This was a modern-day miracle, at least in my eyes. The reason it was a miracle was because I wasn't supposed to be graduating from anything in life. After all, I had never succeeded at much and was not very good at anything. I wasn't supposed to make it.

> The devil knows when someone is going to be used by the Lord, and he will try very hard to stop you before you ever get started.

From the ages of thirteen through eighteen, I struggled with drinking alcohol, getting into a lot of fights, not showing up at school, and just about every other kind of trouble there was. I was becoming a very hard young man, and I was battling the confusion and pain of being sexually abused as a child, multiple times, by both men and women. I battled the pain of rejection from many people; I was told from a very young age that I wasn't going to make it, and that I would end up in prison. I had no direction or goals for my life. I had so many words (seeds) spoken over my life that were coming to pass in negative ways. Those words were essentially curses that were playing out in my life, and I didn't know how to stop them. When you think about it, all fruit comes from a seed that has been in the soil a long time, and when we see bad fruit, we can easily jump to conclusions and point our fingers without knowing what a person has gone through over the course of their life.

The devil tried to take me out between the ages of five and nine years old through molestation, rape, and generational curses that had plagued my family for generations. Every one of those seeds I mentioned was sent by the Enemy to try to destroy me at a very young age. After all, the devil knows when someone is going to be used by the Lord, and he will try very hard to stop you before you ever get started. That's why I really can't stand him—he is nothing but an interrupter. He wants to be an author; however, heaven never gave him a pen. He might be able to read parts of our story, but he can't write our story unless we let him. I'm so glad that I surrendered control of my pen to the Lord and began to let Him write my story. When I say the odds were stacked against me, that's exactly the way it was. If you can relate to odds being stacked against you, I encourage you to begin to talk to yourself with the Word of God! It's the most powerful and creative force we have available to us!

When it seems like the odds are stacked against you, tell yourself the truth and declare out loud who you are in Christ! This list of Bible verses is borrowed from Freedom In Christ Ministries[3], from the New American Standard version of the Bible.

---

3. "Who I Am in Christ." Freedom in Christ Ministries. Accessed April 3, 2023. https://www.ficm.org/about-us/who-i-am-in-christ.

CHAPTER 2: WHEN THE ODDS ARE AGAINST YOU

I am accepted by Him

- I am God's child. (John 1:12)
- As a disciple, I am a friend of Jesus Christ. (John 15:15)
- I have been justified by faith and have peace with God. (Romans 5:1)
- I am united with the Lord, and I am one with Him in spirit. (1 Corinthians 6:17)
- I have been bought with a price, and I belong to God. (1 Corinthians 6:19-20)
- I am a member of Christ's body. (1 Corinthians 12:27)
- I have been chosen by God and adopted as His child. (Ephesians 1:3-8)
- I have been redeemed and forgiven of all my sins. (Colossians 1:13-14)
- I am complete in Christ. (Colossians 2:9-10)
- I have direct access to the throne of grace through Jesus Christ. (Hebrews 4:14-16)

I am secure in Him

- I am free from condemnation. (Romans 8:1-2)
- I am assured that God works for my good in all circumstances. (Romans 8:28)
- I have been established, anointed, and sealed by God. (2 Corinthians 1:21-22)

OVERCOMING GIANTS IN YOUR LIFE

- I am hidden with Christ in God. (Colossians 3:1-4)
- I am confident that God will complete the good work He started in me. (Philippians 1:6)
- I am a citizen of heaven. (Philippians 3:20)
- I have not been given a spirit of fear, but of power, love, and a sound mind. (2 Timothy 1:7)
- I am born of God, and the evil one cannot touch me. (1 John 5:18)

I am significant

- I am a branch of Jesus Christ, the True Vine, and a channel of His life. (John 15:5)
- I have been chosen and appointed to bear fruit. (John 15:16)
- I am God's temple. (1 Corinthians 3:16)
- I am a minister of reconciliation for God. (2 Corinthians 5:17-21)
- I am seated with Jesus Christ in the heavenly realm. (Ephesians 2:6)
- I am God's workmanship. (Ephesians 2:10)
- I may approach God with freedom and confidence. (Ephesians 3:12)
- I can do all things through Christ who strengthens me. (Philippians 4:13)

CHAPTER 2: WHEN THE ODDS ARE AGAINST YOU

Personal Observation

When it seems like the odds are stacked against you, are you willing to confront your history and let Jesus Christ turn it into HIStory? In the previous chapter, you wrote about the giant you are currently facing. Pray and ask God for His perspective and truth concerning that, and for the strategy He wants you to employ right now for this situation.

_____

_____

_____

_____

Personal Prayer

Father, I know that You are for me and not against me. Thank You for making me feel secure and significant. You see me blessed and highly favored. Thank You that I'm connected to You. I can do all things through You because You will give me strength. Amen.

Chapter 3

ROCK BOTTOM

At the age of eighteen, I met the girl who helped me find a relationship with God and showed me a better way of life. She eventually became my wife, and we have been married for nearly thirty years! At the beginning of my senior year of high school, I was invited to a church service. As the preacher was speaking, he looked right at me and said, "Son, God will forgive you, and wants to forgive you of your sins." In arrogance, I mocked it at first, but a few moments later, I responded to an altar call given by that same preacher. I didn't know much about God, but I knew I wanted to be forgiven of my sins because I had a lot of them piled up against me. I was quite good at being a sinner.

At that point, I had not yet hit my breaking point. I was not ready to surrender my life totally to God. After all, I was only eighteen and had not quite lived all the life I wanted to live yet. It wasn't until four months after I graduated from high school that I hit rock bottom. My breaking point came on the night of

OVERCOMING GIANTS IN YOUR LIFE

September 30, 1993, at 10:45 p.m., when I was lying on the couch in the living room. I received a call from my aunt saying that my mom had been rushed to the hospital and that I needed to get there quickly. When I arrived at St. Elizabeth's Hospital around 11:30 p.m., my aunt met me at the door and told me that my mom had been stabbed. They didn't know if she was going to make it. I began to cry out to God and beg Him to keep her alive. So many thoughts raced through my mind in a matter of minutes: *Who did this to my mom? Is my mom going to live? Who is going to raise my three younger brothers and my sister? Why would God allow this to happen?*

We waited for what seemed like an eternity for a response from the doctor in the emergency room. Finally, the doctor came out, and I could tell from the look on his face that my mom didn't make it. Sure enough, he spoke the words I dreaded to hear: "I'm so sorry, but she didn't make it." They tried reviving her for an hour. I later learned that my mom had died before she reached the hospital. This was told to me by the sheriff that responded to the 911 call. She had died at the scene. My mom was murdered by her boyfriend and stabbed seventeen times in front of my younger brother and sister who were seven and nine years old at the time. My little brother tried to fight off her killer. Her killer chased my little sister, who was only nine years old, out of the house with a butcher knife.

CHAPTER 3: ROCK BOTTOM

One month earlier, the same guy stabbed my mom one inch away from her heart. He did thirty days in the Yakima County Jail and then got out and went back to finish what he said he would do. He told her, "If I can't be with you, no one will be with you." He was a jealous man who was highly addicted to drugs and alcohol. The night I found out that he was in her house, after she had taken him back, I went to her home and personally laid hands on him, if you know what I mean.

> The Holy Spirit who helped you conquer your Goliath will empower you to overcome every giant sent your way.

At the age of nineteen, I was faced with too much responsibility; I was overwhelmed with hatred in my heart toward the man who had killed my mom. The night it happened, my uncles, my cousins, and I looked for him for three hours; it is a good thing that we didn't find him then because I probably would have ended up in prison myself. The next morning, they found the guy who did it; he turned himself in to the police. The guy who killed my mom served seventeen years of a twenty-five-year sentence, after being re-sentenced many years later.

OVERCOMING GIANTS IN YOUR LIFE

Later in David's life, other giants showed up to war against him. What is wild is that all of them were related to Goliath! Some of them were Goliath's children and one was his brother (1 Chronicles 20). So after defeating a giant once, David had to face another giant. The Holy Spirit who helped you conquer your Goliath will empower you to overcome every giant sent your way.

This is exactly what happened in our lives. We thought it was a done deal. I thought Goliath was dead, and I could finally move past it. Almost fifteen years later, the case resurfaced. I was confused. Many times in life, things may not go the way we hoped or prayed. When the guy that killed my mom appealed his case because of a law that was passed by our governor, he was able to get his sentence reduced by over eight years. I was ticked. We were all ticked. How could this be? Our justice system is broken. After all, I appreciate God's mercy in my life, but I really battled my mom's murderer receiving God's mercy in his life. That was a hard thing because our family had to peel back the bandage of all that pain and relive it. The wound that had healed over the years had been reopened.

This is where the Holy Spirit truly began to rewrite my story! The night I faced my mountain of sin and pain that needed to be removed and forgiven is when my spiritual journey really began. That night

CHAPTER 3: ROCK BOTTOM

is when my life began to change for the better. It was still an uphill battle, but the Holy Spirit was in my life now. I still had a ton of hurdles to jump, but I was determined to follow God's plan. I had a great support team around me; they helped me and were there for me—I needed it.

One of the biggest challenges of my life was facing in court the man that killed my mom. I had to face him at the trial—from fourteen feet away—and he asked me in front of a room full of my family, friends, and the media, to forgive him for murdering my mom. That was a defining moment for me in my walk with God—to face that man and look him square in the eyes, and be able to say, "Yes, I forgive you." I had to do this with so much pressure coming from so many hurting hearts that did not understand how I could forgive the man that did this. At that moment, I did not feel like forgiving him, but I knew that I needed to forgive him—for myself and my family who needed to see the real Jesus. Forgiveness is one of the most powerful forces in life. The thought that was going through my mind was: *Yes, I will forgive you by faith*; but as I said yes to him that day, that hour, it was like a million pounds were lifted off of my shoulders.

I learned something very important that day; when you forgive someone, you set a prisoner free, and often, that prisoner is you. FORGIVENESS DOESN'T MAKE THE OTHER PERSON RIGHT;

OVERCOMING GIANTS IN YOUR LIFE

IT MAKES YOU FREE. Was this forgiveness a once and done deal for me? No, it wasn't. I would have to continually say to myself, hundreds of times over the next few years, "I forgive Nelson." However, the moment that I faced my own personal Goliath was the moment my own path to healing began.

Personal Observation

When it seems like you just can't forgive, you need to remember how much you have been forgiven! Is there anyone that you need to forgive right now? Write down their names and say out loud that you forgive them.

_____

_____

_____

_____

_____

_____

_____

_____

_____

_____

_____

CHAPTER 3: ROCK BOTTOM

Personal Prayer

Father, thank You for forgiving me. I know that I need to be better at forgiving others. Holy Spirit, help me to be able to forgive and receive Your healing power in my life. Lead me not into temptation, and deliver me from evil. As I forgive others, I know that You will forgive me. Amen.

Chapter 4

GOD ENCOUNTERS

The years 1993 and 1994 were drastically different for me because I had received Christ into my life! Just a few weeks after losing my mom, I was still struggling to give up drinking and partying with all of my friends. I wanted to live for God, but the pull from the other side was intense. Because I was living with one foot in the kingdom and one foot in the world, I didn't have peace, and the Enemy still had access and authority in my life. One thing I know now is that your past can only hold onto you if you're holding onto it. Within one month, I experienced three major encounters with God's power, love, and having a sound mind. It's crucial to have the right people around you; a lot of people can't appreciate your breakthroughs because they don't know or understand your "beenthroughs." We are so good at judging someone's glory when we don't know their story. I have always said, "You cannot write my prescription if you don't know my pain."

I remember walking home from a party one night; I was drunk and praying for God to help me. When I got home, I watched a Benny Hinn miracle crusade in my room. I was still drunk. I was buzzing good, if you know what I mean. I got down on my knees and said, "Jesus, please take this alcohol from me." I kid you not; five minutes later, the preacher said through the TV, "Right now, God is setting a young man free from alcohol, and you will never touch it again." When he said that, I felt something that I had never felt before—a power that I had never experienced in my life. The room instantly stopped spinning, and I was sober, as if I had not been drunk that night. It felt like electricity going through my entire body. Friends, that was thirty years ago, and I'm still free today! I immediately called my girlfriend who had been praying that God would reveal Himself to me. She didn't want to break up with me; she was afraid that I wouldn't let her date anyone else—that I would beat them up. She was probably right! I didn't know it then, but she and her parents were praying that night for God to save me. I'm so glad that He saved me. That is when God gave me a sound mind!

During that same time period, my mother's funeral was to take place, and it was very important for me to have my mom buried close to a high school friend of mine who had lost his life in a car accident. I remember praying for God to allow this to happen. When we pulled into the cemetery, and I saw the place that my mom was going to be buried, my eyes filled with tears of joy and peace; she would be buried within fifteen feet of my high school friend. I knew that only God

CHAPTER 4: GOD ENCOUNTERS

could answer a prayer like that. After all, I was the only person who knew that He answered my prayer that day because I had only prayed it the night before! That was where I encountered God's Power! If you are struggling to believe that He answers prayer, do what I did, and pray a prayer that only you and God know about. When He answers it, you will know that He is REAL!

> **If you are struggling to believe that God answers prayer, pray a prayer that only you and God know about. When He answers it, you will know that He is REAL!**

God was working in my heart, but the devil was whispering in my ear. I was asked to attend a gospel crusade at the SunDome in Yakima. The preacher was coming all the way from Florida, and I had never seen him or heard him speak before. At the end of his message, he asked for everyone under twenty-five years of age to come down to the front. So I went forward. There where hundreds of people at the altar. He prayed for two girls, and then he looked right at me and started to pray for me. My heart was racing. The words that he spoke that night were given to him by God. He said, "Because you lost your mother, the devil is trying his best to take you back. He knows he has lost you and wants you back." He told me other things in that moment that only God

OVERCOMING GIANTS IN YOUR LIFE

and my very close friends and family knew. It was a life-changing moment. After all, for God to send someone all the way across the country to share something like that with me blew my mind. It made me realize that He loved me and had a great plan for my life—a plan that I didn't realize. I knew that I had just encountered the real love of Jesus Christ!

April 9, 1994, was the day that I married the girl I have been talking about: Kari Johnson. That day forever changed my legacy and my life! Not long after we were married, Kari and I were both called into ministry. We became youth pastors and served in that capacity for the next ten years. We reached out to many kids who were just like I was. To this day, we still reach out to as many people as possible, with the love of God, through outreaches all over our city. God was really working in my life and revealing His will for me. From 1995 to 2003, we served God in the same church where I gave my heart to Him. In 1999, I also started working in a prison as a corrections officer and did that for five years. I think it's amazing, when I look back now, to see that the words that were spoken over my life had come to pass. Instead of being in prison, which easily could have happened, I was working in a prison and talking to guys about Jesus all the time. Only God could do that! It's what I now call a *but-God moment* that happened in my life.

In 2003, Kari and I were asked to take over the church that my in-laws had started. At that time in my

CHAPTER 4: GOD ENCOUNTERS

life, I didn't want to be a senior pastor. I saw some of the things that pastors go through, and honestly, it scared me big time! So, in my stubborn way, I began to pray for an escape route out of Yakima. I was born and raised here, but at that time, I wanted out badly. So God, in His permissible will, opened the door for a youth pastor job in Federal Way, Washington. We accepted the position, and we were off to the west side of the state. We lived there from 2004 to 2006. Because I was running from the will of God for my life, and had lots of pain that had not been dealt with, God used those two years to teach me that His way is always better. The west side for me was a whale's-belly experience, just like Jonah in the Bible. I know now that when you run from God's call on your life, He will always have a big fish prepared for you! God had to deal with me.

My wife and I, through prayer and wrestling with God over His plan for our lives, began to be more desperate for God's will than our own will. In prayer, God began to speak to my wife from the book of Nehemiah, about how Nehemiah went back to his home that lied in ruins, to rebuild the city walls. At first, I didn't want to hear it because the last thing I wanted was to go back to a city that contained so many painful memories for me. After a few weeks of praying, God began to deal with us both about the transition. We tried to talk Him into sending us to Texas or California, but He wasn't listening. I think my next book should be about Jonah! After all, I have some life experience that has helped me to completely relate with him also!

As we continued to read the Bible, it became very apparent that God was saying, "I want you to return to Yakima to help rebuild the walls of that city." As we prayed for confirmation, He opened the door for us to move back to Yakima. What was incredible to me was that I used to drive out of Yakima and say, "Thank you, Jesus." Because I had so much pain associated with my home town, I didn't have His heart for it. But after He changed my heart, I found myself driving back into Yakima saying, "Thank you, Jesus." In 2006, we moved back to Yakima; and in 2007, we took over leadership of the church that we were running away from pastoring two years earlier. I think about how the Bible says that the word of the LORD came to Jonah a second time! I'm so thankful that He gave me a second chance! One thing I learned during that process is that God won't make you do anything that you don't want to do; He will just make you wish that you had done it!

There are clear instructions in the book of Nehemiah about having the king's blessing to go back to the city. We also felt that we should talk to the pastor of the church we were serving at the time and ask for his blessing; that was important to us. When we talked with him about returning to Yakima, he told us he would give us his blessing if we would go and pastor the church in Yakima. Once that happened, we knew that God was

CHAPTER 4: GOD ENCOUNTERS

sending us back to the place we had run away from. In 2007, we became the pastors of what is now Breakthrough Church here in Yakima. We love our church; we love our city; and we have been pastoring at Breakthrough ever since. We have seen God do some amazing things in this city. We have helped thousands of people in their relationship with God, and we will continue to share the good news with everyone that we can.

Just a few words of encouragement:

- Pastor Jim Raley said, "In life, never be ashamed of your scars; they prove you lived through everything that tried to kill you. When God promoted David, He gave him a lion, a bear, a Samuel, a Goliath, a Saul, a cave, a Jonathan, mighty men—and then a crown."

- Pastor Jim also said, "Your wounds reveal that the devil may have tried, but he did not defeat you. Even if he hit you with his best shot, God has given and will give you the victory."

- A curse may have run in your family; however, it stops with you!

- God will bring to you people who need to hear about your past so it won't become their future.

- Keep reaching into the river of God's grace to pick up your smooth stones; after all, they will need to be your weapons of choice.

OVERCOMING GIANTS IN YOUR LIFE

Personal Observation

What has God done in your life that you need to praise Him for?

_____

_____

_____

_____

Personal Prayer

Father, thank You for working miracles in my life. I know that because of Your grace, I am a miracle! Help me to always remember what You have done in my life and to always be grateful for it. I never want to be ungrateful. Lord, I want to encounter Your love and power every day of my life from this day forward. Amen.

Chapter 5

STONES AND STEPS

We all love to read the story of David and Goliath, and here is where it gets very practical. It is actually much more than just a story; it is an outline of God's principles for success in overcoming any type of giant. Let's break it down; but first, read these words from Max Lucado and get ready to learn how to overcome the giants in your life!

> "There are certain things that everyone knows not to do. You don't fight a lion with a toothpick. You don't go bear hunting with a paint ball gun. And you don't send a shepherd boy to battle a ten-foot giant. You don't, that is, unless you're out of options. Saul was. And it's when we're out of options that we are most ready for God's surprises."

> "Was Saul ever surprised! The king tried to give David some equipment. *What do you want, boy? Shield? Sword?*

OVERCOMING GIANTS IN YOUR LIFE

Grenades? Rifles? God's most powerful tools are the simplest. David had something else in mind: five smooth stones and an ordinary leather sling. The soldiers gasped. Saul sighed. Goliath mocked. David swung. And God made His point. Anyone who underestimates what God can do with the ordinary, has rocks in his head!"[4]

We read that David chose for himself five smooth stones and put them in his bag. He then ran toward the giant—unafraid. Just like David had five smooth stones, God also gave me five stones that I would like to share with you in this chapter.

I have heard it said that the five smooth stones spelled J-E-S-U-S. After all, He is the Rock of our salvation!

Smooth Stone #1 – My relationship with Jesus Christ // It changed everything for me, my family, and my future

You must have a personal relationship with Jesus if you are going to overcome giants. In fact, it's the only way!

---

4. Lucado, Max. "God Makes His Point." Max Lucado, August 27, 2015. https://maxlucado.com/listen/god-makes-his-point/.

CHAPTER 5: STONES AND STEPS

 Step 1: If you're going to defeat your enemies, you can't hang out with them.

There must be a valley between you and them. Pastor Benny Perez said in his book *Upside Down*, "There was a distinction between the two armies. There was no question as to which army a person served because of the distance between the two sides."[5] Today, the forces of darkness are gathered to wage war against us. There were two distinct sides in David's time; there are also two separate kingdoms at war in our own day. We cannot be in both armies. You must choose which side you're on! Choose God's side! We are either serving in the army of God or the army of Satan. God wants us to be HOT (fervent) or COLD (self-absorbed) because being lukewarm is completely unacceptable (Revelation 3:16). Choose today which side you're going to be on!

> The Philistines stood on a mountain on one side, and Israel stood on a mountain on the other side, with a valley between them. (1 Samuel 17:3)

Conviction is useless until it's converted to conduct.

---

[5]. Perez, Benny. *Upside down: A Guidebook for Global Impact*. Lake Mary, FL: Charisma House, 2003, 79.

OVERCOMING GIANTS IN YOUR LIFE

 Step 2: You must believe that no matter how big your enemy is, your God is much greater.

Your greatest weapon is not what you can do to your enemy, but rather what you can become when you're in the presence of the One who has never been intimidated by the Enemy. The Enemy looks much smaller in the secret place than he does on the battlefield. Remember, Goliath was between nine and eleven feet tall, weighed between 500 and 600 pounds, and wore armor totaling around 230 pounds.

> And a champion went out from the camp of the Philistines, named Goliath, from Gath, whose height was six cubits and a span. He had a bronze helmet on his head, and he was armed with a coat of mail, and the weight of the coat was five thousand shekels of bronze. (1 Samuel 17:4-5)

The next time you feel like telling God how big your problems are, try telling your problems how big your GOD is.

CHAPTER 5: STONES AND STEPS

 Step 3: Use your sword.

No matter how dangerous your enemies' spears and threats may seem, you have a sword, and you must know how to use it.

> Now the staff of his spear was like a weaver's beam, and his iron spearhead weighed six hundred shekels; and a shield-bearer went before him. (1 Samuel 17:7)

> For the word of God *is* living and powerful, and sharper than any two-edged sword, piercing even to the division of soul and spirit, and of joints and marrow, and is a discerner of the thoughts and intents of the heart. (Hebrews 4:12)

Goliath's first mistake—devils don't intimidate the Holy Spirit; they are subject to Him.

OVERCOMING GIANTS IN YOUR LIFE

 Step 4: Step it up in the moment.

When everybody else around you is afraid to arise, you must be the one to seize the moment and become a warrior. I believe David understood that battlefields of obedience lead to battlefields of significance. God measures our success by our obedience. I want to encourage you to think big in small places; and watch, small places will become big places.

> When Saul and all Israel heard these words of the Philistine, they were dismayed and greatly afraid. (1 Samuel 17:11)

 **Smooth Stone #2 – My Outlook // David's outlook was different**

Israel had never heard of David until he stood toe-to-toe with Goliath. To the rest of Israel, Goliath appeared to be a ten-foot wall. For forty days, they stared at the wall and hoped it would go away. David saw things differently. Where others saw a wall, David saw a door. And because he ventured through the threshold, God gave him access to a whole new level of favor and opportunity.

> Then as he talked with them, there was the champion, the Philistine of Gath, Goliath by name, coming up from

CHAPTER 5: STONES AND STEPS

the armies of the Philistines; and he spoke according to the same words. So David heard them. And all the men of Israel, when they saw the man, fled from him and were dreadfully afraid. So the men of Israel said, "Have you seen this man who has come up? Surely he has come up to defy Israel; and it shall be that the man who kills him the king will enrich with great riches, will give him his daughter, and give his father's house exemption from taxes in Israel." (1 Samuel 17:23-25)

Smooth Stone #3 – My Courage // David's courage was different

David understood that whoever messed with him messed with God because of the covenant!

 Step 5: Your motives must be pure.

Sometimes Jesus isn't all you need until He's all you've got. Make sure you are hearing right! Listen to the voice of God, and He will correct your motives!

> Then David spoke to the men who stood by him, saying, "What shall be done for the man who kills this Philistine and takes away the reproach from Israel? For

who is this uncircumcised Philistine, that he should defy the armies of the living God?" (1 Samuel 17:26)

 Step 6: You must remind yourself that it really doesn't matter what others think of you.

"David's brothers did not think he had warrior potential. King Saul did not think David had champion potential."[6]

> Now Eliab his oldest brother heard when he spoke to the men; and Eliab's anger was aroused against David, and he said, "Why did you come down here? And with whom have you left those few sheep in the wilderness? I know your pride and the insolence of your heart, for you have come down to see the battle." (1 Samuel 17:28)

> Then David said to Saul, "Let no man's heart fail because of him; your servant will go and fight with this Philistine." And Saul said to David, "You are not able to go against this Philistine to fight with him; for you are a youth, and he a man of war from his youth." (1 Samuel 17:32-33)

---

6. Maxwell, John. *Running With The Giants*. New York, NY: Faith Words, 2002, 41-42.

CHAPTER 5: STONES AND STEPS

> "Your servant has killed both lion and bear; and this uncircumcised Philistine will be like one of them, seeing he has defied the armies of the living God." (1 Samuel 17:36)

 Step 7: You must remember your past victories.

They will increase your faith for future trials and temptations. Most people think the lion and bear were trying to stop David from fulfilling his destiny, but they were his destiny!

> Moreover David said, "The LORD, who delivered me from the paw of the lion and from the paw of the bear, He will deliver me from the hand of this Philistine." (1 Samuel 17:37)

Max Lucado said,

> "We must surround ourselves with the memories of how God parted our Red Seas and killed our Goliaths. Every time we come to a new river or a new giant, we will surge forward with a future confidence inspired by past victories. We must intentionally record God's faithfulness; this ensures that the success God gave us

OVERCOMING GIANTS IN YOUR LIFE

yesterday doesn't get lost in the uncertainty of today.

"Satan has no recourse to your personal testimony. Your best weapon against his attacks is a good memory!

- Don't forget God's blessings
- He forgives your sins—every one of them
- He heals your diseases—every one of them
- He redeems you from hell—and saves your life
- He crowns you with love and mercy—a paradise crown
- He renews your youth—you're always young in his presence

"Create a trophy room in your heart, and place a memory on the shelf. Before you face a challenge, take a quick tour of God's accomplishments on your behalf. Look at all the paychecks He's provided, all the blessings He's given, and all the prayers He's answered.

"Imitate the shepherd boy, David. Before he fought Goliath, the giant, he remembered how God had helped him kill a lion

CHAPTER 5: STONES AND STEPS

and a bear. Face your future by recalling God's victories! It truly is vital!"[7]

 Step 8: Know the Enemy's tactics

Be aware that just before you're about to do something great for God, the Enemy will send somebody your way to try to put something on you that is not from God, i.e. their armor, their beliefs about you, their religion, their rules, etc. What do you need to take off or remove from your life?

> David fastened his sword to his armor and tried to walk, for he had not tested them. And David said to Saul, "I cannot walk with these, for I have not tested them." So David took them off. (1 Samuel 17:39)

 Step 9: Your methods must be sure.

David used what he was good with: stones and a sling!

> Then he took his staff in his hand; and **he chose for himself five smooth stones from the brook**, and put them in a

---
7. Lucado, Max. "Your Best Weapon against Satan." Max Lucado, June 16, 2016. https://maxlucado.com/listen/your-best-weapon-against-satan.

shepherd's bag, in a pouch which he had, and his sling was in his hand. And he drew near to the Philistine. (1 Samuel 17:40)

So the Philistine said to David, "Am I a dog, that you come to me with sticks?" And the Philistine cursed David by his gods. And the Philistine said to David, "Come to me, and I will give your flesh to the birds of the air and the beasts of the field!" (1 Samuel 17:43-44)

 Step 10: You must be able to stand in the face of opposition.

"Goliath did not think David even had opponent potential. You can easily determine the caliber of a person by the amount of opposition it takes to discourage him or her. David faced great opposition. Everyone told David he had no potential, but he was able to:

- Go beyond his family (relational limitations)
- Go beyond King Saul (leadership limitations)
- Go beyond the lion, the bear, and Goliath (skill limitations)"[8]

Then David said to the Philistine, "You come to me with a sword, with a spear, and with a javelin. But I come to you

---

8. Maxwell, John. *Running With The Giants*. New York, NY: Faith Words, 2002, 41-42.

CHAPTER 5: STONES AND STEPS

in the name of the LORD of hosts, the God of the armies of Israel, whom you have defied." (1 Samuel 17:45)

Smooth Stone #4 – My Declaration // You must open your mouth and speak to your giant

Goliath doesn't want you to know how to defeat him with his own sword. You do this by refusing his condemnation, his guilt, his shame, and his lies.

The anointing does not protect us FROM the fight; it protects us IN the fight.

 Step 11: You're going to have to prophesy to the giants standing before you!

Goliath wants to foretell your future. Fear tries to do the same thing to us; it tries to foul up our future by paralyzing our present.

> This day the LORD will deliver you into my hand, and I will strike you and take your head from you. And this day I will give the carcasses of the camp of the Philistines to the birds of the air and to the wild beasts of

the earth, that all the earth may know that there is a God in Israel. (1 Samuel 17:46)

 Step 12: You must remember that your strength comes from the Lord.

David was assured that the Lord was with him and would help him to prevail over the giant.

> Then all this assembly shall know that the LORD does not save with sword and spear; for the battle is the LORD's, and He will give you into our hands. (1 Samuel 17:47)

> I can do all things through Christ who gives me strength. (Philippians 4:13)

 Step 13: You don't need to know as much about your enemy as what the Holy Spirit is saying about your enemy.

In fact, the Holy Spirit doesn't respond when our focus is the Enemy—He responds when He is our focus. Your dilemma doesn't have to stop you dead in your tracks. It can become the gateway to another dimension of God's activity in your life. So make sure that you are looking to the Holy Spirit!

> So it was, when the Philistine arose and came and drew near to meet David, that David hurried and ran toward the army to

CHAPTER 5: STONES AND STEPS

> meet the Philistine. Then David put his hand in his bag and took out a stone; and he slung it and struck the Philistine in his forehead, so that the stone sank into his forehead, and he fell on his face to the earth. (1 Samuel 17:48-49)

 Step 14: There must not be any hesitation on your part.

Don't open the door for the devil. You must know that the devil will always try to make provision for your procrastination, but God will provide passion for your prevailing. God is going to give somebody back their passion! I believe that if the rock in David's sling could talk, that rock would have asked, *Why am I here? Why am I alone? Why am I going backward?* All this, right before being propelled into victory! You might feel exactly like that rock at this moment in your life. I declare over your life that you are not stuck. You are found and favored by God! Whatever you do in this time in your life, just make sure you are moving! A parked car won't go anywhere until you put it in drive. Get moving! There is a very powerful principle in the book of Exodus: God fights for us as we move!

> So David prevailed over the Philistine with a sling and a stone and struck the Philistine and killed him. But there was no sword in the hand of David. Therefore

OVERCOMING GIANTS IN YOUR LIFE

David ran and stood over the Philistine, took his sword and drew it out of its sheath and killed him, and cut off his head with it. And when the Philistines saw that their champion was dead, they fled. (1 Samuel 17:50-51)

Smooth Stone #5 – My Purpose // Your purpose is revealed in your testimony

After you defeat your giant, you must carry your victory around with you wherever you go, and keep telling your story because it's the greatest way to get ahead (A Head!)

> Therefore David ran and stood over the Philistine, took his sword, and drew it out of its sheath and killed him, and cut off his head with it. And David took the head of the Philistine and brought it to Jerusalem, but he put his armor in his tent. (1 Samuel 17:51, 54)

The following scripture has helped me along the way:

> And we know that all things work together for good to those who love God, to those who are the called according to *His* purpose. (Romans 8:28)

CHAPTER 5: STONES AND STEPS

I say that if what you're going through isn't good yet, then God's not done yet! Hang in there! He can and will turn it around if you let Him! God is no respecter of persons; He is, however, a respecter of those who have a relationship with Him! The LORD has blessed my life in ways I didn't think were possible:

- I have three amazing daughters and a son-in-law!
- I have been married to my high school sweetheart for nearly thirty years!
- I have been in ministry for twenty-eight years!
- I get to pastor an amazing church called Breakthrough Church in my home state of Washington!
- Jesus continues to rescue people with the message of the gospel through my life and my testimony!
- I have seen thousands of people come to faith in Christ because I surrendered my life to Him in 1994.
- I'm not ashamed of the gospel of Jesus Christ!

Just like David chose smooth stones from the brook, it will be vital for you to also have weapons that you fight with. These are the smooth stones that, by the grace of God, I have been able to use in my life! I encourage you to think back over your own life and remember all that God has done and will continue to do for you!

OVERCOMING GIANTS IN YOUR LIFE

Personal Observation

Now that you know my story, write down your story. I'd love to read it and say a prayer for you. Please email me at brian@breakthroughchristian.com

_____
_____
_____
_____
_____
_____
_____
_____
_____
_____
_____
_____
_____
_____
_____
_____
_____
_____

CHAPTER 5: STONES AND STEPS

Benediction Prayer

Father, thank You for continuing to make a way for me in my life! Help me to realize the smooth stones that You have made available to me! I will always look to You as my Source, my Provider, my Defender, and my HOPE! Thank You for working everything together for my good! Thank You for healing my life in a powerful way! Thank You for the good news of the gospel: that with Jesus Christ in my life, I have king potential, warrior potential, champion potential, and opponent potential; and because of that, I can and will OVERCOME GIANTS IN MY LIFE in Jesus's mighty name! Amen.

ABOUT THE AUTHOR

Brian is the lead pastor of Breakthrough Church in Union Gap, Washington. He has been ordained since 2002 and has ministered as a pastor for over twenty-eight years. Brian is committed to demonstrating and advancing the kingdom of God centered around Jesus Christ and empowered by the Holy Spirit to reach this generation that is asleep spiritually and searching for their purpose. He believes in equipping and releasing every person into the call God has placed on their lives. Brian and his wife, Kari, have three daughters and a son-in-law who all serve in the church. Brian can be contacted at brian@breakthroughchristian.com.

WORKS CITED

1. Maxwell, John. *Running With The Giants*. New York, NY: Faith Words, 2002, 40.
2. Hearn Travis. *Shaq Sized Problems Require God Sized Miracles*, n.d. Nov 27, 2013, Sermon Central Article.
3. 3. *Who I Am in Christ*. Freedom in Christ Ministries. Accessed April 3, 2023. https://www.ficm.org/about-us/who-i-am-in-christ/.
4. 4. Lucado, Max. *God Makes His Point*. Max Lucado, August 27, 2015. https://maxlucado.com/listen/god-makes-his-point/.
5. Perez, Benny. *Upside down: A Guidebook for Global Impact*. Lake Mary, FL: Charisma House, 2003, 79.
6. Maxwell, John. *Running With The Giants*. New York, NY: Faith Words, 2002, 41-42.
7. Lucado, Max. *Your Best Weapon against Satan*. Max Lucado, June 16, 2016. https://maxlucado.com/listen/your-best-weapon-against-satan/.
8. Maxwell, John. *Running With The Giants*. New York, NY: Faith Words, 2002, 41-42.

Made in the USA
Monee, IL
07 June 2023